Table of Contents

D1696885

What is this Book About Anyway?

When you think of artificial intelligence (A.I.), what do you usually think of? My guess is that it is something close to *Terminator* or *Ultron*. Now when you think of data, what comes to mind? Are they pictures of spreadsheets and raw numbers? You are probably asking yourself right now, "How are these two even remotely connected?" In this book, we will explore the wonders of artificial intelligence, but in conjunction with that, how data is also a factor into the creation of such wonderful machines.

Before we even begin to discuss A.I., we should first take a step back and look at what we have been able to accomplish before. This way, we will get a better sense of how powerful modern A.I. implementations are compared to their predecessors. There are three iterations we will cover, so let us jump right into it.

First Iteration

The first iteration is "rules-based" where computers performed tasks based on rules. Think of games like pong. If we build a program that plays pong in this iteration, the paddle will move up when the ball moves up, and the paddle will move down when the ball moves down. These rules are *hardcoded* into the program, which tells us already a lot about their limitations.

Can you think of one limitation? One limitation is that they do not have room for improvement. They are static and not dynamic. This means that once this machine gets programmed, it does not improve itself anymore as everything is deterministic. Think of studying for a math test where you solely focused on rote studying one practice exam. Come the actual test, all the problems that you know how to solve are only those that you saw in the practice exam. In this scenario, you did not actually learn the process of finding a solution.

This becomes problematic when it comes to language translation. Language requires context in both surrounding content, time, place, and others. When you hard code a system to do direct word per word translation, the results do not turn out well. To demonstrate, try translating word per word a sentence from a foreign language to your native tongue. Chances are, the translation will neither be accurate nor grammatically correct.

Second Iteration

We need to do better than hardcoded rules for our systems. If we were to create self-driving cars, listing all the rules will be arduous, inefficient, and lacking. It becomes burdensome to write all those scenarios and rules. What if instead of hardcoded rules, we give our machine choices and probabilities?

By giving our machines choices, we can increase our performance and reduce the amount of work that we ourselves would do. Encoding rules and listing all those scenarios that we must account for is both inefficient and a waste of time.

What becomes of our machine is akin to that of a decision tree. You start with a scenario, and then you try to find the best path to your intended goal. For example, instead of translating word per word, you would give your machine choices and then instruct it to find the "best optimal path." This path is our solution to the translation problem.

The problem with this approach is that we are left with the task of uncovering options for our machines. What if we instead made machines that learn from the data itself? That way, we can just spend our time collecting and adjusting the data that it needs. This cuts our time significantly. We are already there.

Third Iteration

The third iteration is now. We have "thinking" machines that do not need specific tinkering from us. We code up a generalized algorithm, feed it data, and it performs the task we assign it to do. Want the machine to tell the difference between a cat and a dog? Feed the algorithm pictures of cats and dogs and it will learn the pattern. What about classifying between chairs and tables? Follow the same process as above. The task that we are left to do in the third iteration is to find the data, as opposed to thinking of hundreds or even thousands of possible scenarios, rules, or options for our machine's internal decision making process.

A popular example of this in the gaming world is OpenAI's DotA bot. DotA, otherwise known as Defense of the Ancients, is a multiplayer game in which two competing teams comprise of up to five members. The objective of the game is to destroy the Ancient—the main tower of the opposing team—at the other side of the map. There are a lot of variables at play in this game. For example, there are three main lanes in the map, each comprising of three towers in sequence. Before you could even destroy the opponent's Ancient, your team would have to destroy these towers. Now of course, this is optional, as you could probably charge your way into the enemy's base. The downside of that is that, if not strong enough, you would probably die. Moreover, you have creatures called "creeps" that are generated per specific time interval that attack the opposing team in sight. You would have to deal with those as well. Finally, there are the members of the opposing team that you would have to deal with. These are just some of the thousands of other variables you would have to consider in the game—it is complicated, to say the least.

OpenAI is a research company in San Francisco, California. Their goal is to promote and develop friendly A.I. that benefits and helps us, instead of hurting and killing us like what we see in Hollywood movies. Key people in its founding were Tesla and SpaceX CEO Elon Musk and Y Combinator President Sam Altman. OpenAI's DotA bot learned from past games and managed to beat the world's top DotA players in a 1v1 contest. Imagine doing that in the first or second iteration, where you list down all the rules, scenarios, or options you would give your machine in a specific game state. That would take forever.

Artificial General Intelligence

The ultimate goal of the third iteration would be to reach artificial general intelligence (AGI). As we will see later, our current implementations of A.I. only work well within a specified domain. For example, a deep neural network, as we will discuss later on, may work well with identifying credit card fraud, but when you try and make it predict if a person has cancer or not, you would need to build an entirely new deep neural network. As of now, our implementations of A.I. are only knowledgeable within the domain they are trained to learn on.

The eventual goal of A.I. research is to reach AGI, which is one algorithm that can learn anything. Think of it like *Terminator* or *Ultron*. Not only will this algorithm learn the difference between cats and dogs, but it will also learn military strategy, how to poach an egg, and many others. It is this ability to learn from multiple domains at that will enable humanity to reach the next frontier in technological progress.

What's Next?

Hopefully you now have an appreciation of what A.I. is capable of after seeing how lacking previous iterations were. Truth be told, A.I. continues to surprise us every day. New algorithms, methods, optimization techniques, and implementations are being reported every single day. In the succeeding chapters, we will stretch the capabilities of A.I. to their fullest potential by looking at current implementations and possible future implementations.

Think of it this way, the wonders of physics bought us Newton's three laws of motion, Maxwell's equations, Schrödinger's equations, Einstein's relativity, and many others down the line. It has led to manned missions to the moon, the discovery of the Higgs-Boson, the discovery of gravitational waves, SpaceX's reusable engine rockets, and many others. Physics has been in existence for more than 200 years. What about A.I. research? Around less than a quarter of that. The possibilities are endless, which means our imaginations with how we can use A.I. are as well.

How do Machines Learn?

The idea of machines learning from data is astonishing. However, algorithms and computer programs knowing just how to perform a specific task by feeding it data is not unheard of. Ever taken a statistics course? If you have, then do you recall linear regression models?

A linear regression model is a model that finds the best-fitting line by minimizing a cost function. Let us unpack it by looking at the picture below.

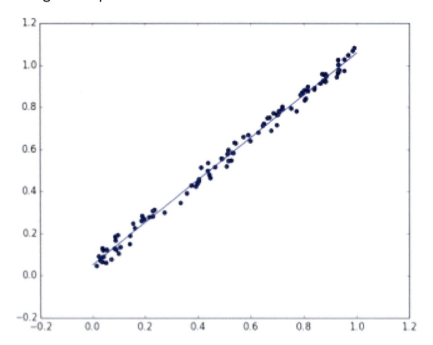

That line you see in the graph tries to fit itself in the best possible way given those scattered data points. For the line to do this, it minimizes a cost function. This cost function tells the line, "this is how much it is costing you if your orientation looks like that." With every parameter tweak to best fit the points, the cost function spits out a number. The job of the line is to find that lowest number, which signals the best fit.

This concept is important, as it is used by us and A.I. as well. Think of driving back home to beat the traffic. As you start the engine, you think to yourself, "which routes should I take to get home as fast as possible while avoiding traffic?" Another example is in studying smartly. When you study, do you study the entire textbook, or do you focus your study on what you anticipate your teacher to show during the test? We humans tend to look at patterns and signals in our environment that enable us to better use our time. Our own "cost function" is that little voice in our head saying, "you probably should not waste your time on that."

Once we minimize our cost function by eliminating needless things, then what? How do we learn? This is when we "tune" our hyperparameters. Think of hyperparameters as these knobs in our head that you adjust for us to better fit an idea in our head. An example of this is in cooking. When you are first learning, the combination of your measurements and approximations throughout the cooking session may not be right in your head. Your inner cost function tells you then to "use less water" or "add more salt" next time, with you yourself taking note of these small adjustments. The next time you do it, assuming you took the time to reflect on what your cost function told you, will result in a better dish. You tweaked your cooking by tweaking the "using less water" and "adding more salt" knobs to better yourself.

Another example would be learning the lyrics to a new song. You probably will not remember the entire song after just one listen. But as you continue to listen, you start adding small mental cues and other personal reminders to yourself like "this verse is the introduction" or "this verse comes right after the chorus." Perhaps even getting details because of changed in tone or rhythm by saying "after the B chord in this verse I start the rap" or "after using a vibrato here I can do a freestyle here."

How we learn depends on how good we can learn from our mistakes. But for us to understand that one action in a long chain of actions was a mistake requires a better understanding of our cost functions. These internal functions signal to us how we can better tune these different hyperparameters to speed up learning.

What if we already know our hyperparameters in the long run? All the better! That means that our learning rate can be increased. Think of it like this: before reading a book, you read the book and character summaries and what past readers had to say about the book. This means that before reading the actual book, you already have a sense of what it is going to contain, so mental knobs inside your brain start adjusting in anticipation for that. When you start reading the book, it becomes much easier to absorb as you already have a general idea what to expect. Learning becomes faster this way as you do not need to spend time learning the big picture anymore, but rather can spend time focusing on the little details you pick up that fit into the bigger picture as you read along.

As we can see, how machines learn is just how we learn. We infuse a lot of insights we get into how we humans learn and write programs and mathematical formulations to represent it. We are still far away from AGI, but our current implementations are impressive as they are. However, if someday we want a fully functioning AGI that hopefully does not kill us, we need to dig a little bit deeper and learn more insights as to how we learn and how we interpret that for our machines. Let us cover three types of machine learning: supervised, unsupervised, and reinforcement learning.

Supervised Learning

What do you think of when the word "supervised" comes into mind? Perhaps you opening a door for someone when you know that their hands are full because they are carrying tons of boxes? How about helping your grandparents cross the street? Helping your sibling stand up after he or she tripped during a game you were playing? This general idea of "receiving help" is a good way to understand how supervised learning works.

This "help" in supervised learning comes in the form of knowing the answers beforehand. Let us go back to our math test example from before. It does not make sense for us to study for our upcoming math test and not verify the right answers. If we do not do this, then it might end up with us learning bad habits or imagining that a certain technique works when it does not. What we do instead is we study a practice exam, then cross-validate with the answer key. This way, we can eliminate techniques or concepts that we already mastered so we can better focus on things we lack for the test instead.

For machines, this means giving them learning materials we call "training data." This training data is our set that contains thousands, if not, millions or billions of examples to learn from. This dataset contains the answer of course, because as the A.I. tries to learn from the data, it will cross-validate its own answers from the actual answers to properly tune its own hyperparameters. Think of it like learning to memorize something through flash cards. You try to answer in the best of your abilities what the front side of the flash card is asking for, and then validate at the back to see if your answer was right or not. The A.I. does the same.

After learning from the training dataset, the A.I. is exposed to a testing dataset. This dataset contains instances of examples the A.I. has never seen before. This is done to test if the A.I. learned or if it just managed to memorize the pattern of that training dataset. In a real-life scenario, it is just like that math example we had earlier. Did we really learn from the practice test, not paid enough attentions entirely, or just memorized the solutions? If an A.I. does not perform well, then the A.I. either "underfitted" or "overfitted" its hyperparameters for the training dataset. Underfitting is when you did not learn enough from your training set, while overfitting means just memorizing your training set. Both scenarios cause an A.I. to not perform well.

As you can see, supervised learning requires a lot of examples to work with. Typical A.I. implementations usually work with at least 100,000 instances of data for the predictions in the real world to be as correct as possible. Furthermore, this type of learning assumes a well-defined outcome in the end. What if we are just given learning materials and are not told what to do with it?

Unsupervised Learning

The word unsupervised is the opposite of supervised. If before we thought of "with help," then it logically follows that here we mean "without help." In terms of learning, you are given learning materials without a clearly defined goal in mind. The word "clearly" is used because there may be a goal in mind. Imagine needing to write a poem or a short story. Instead of copying others right off the bat, you read through literature after literature looking at how they structured theirs, how their literary devices were used in relation to the theme, how their theme is relevant at the time they were written, et al. You job is to look for patterns on your own.

Machine can also do the same thing. Earlier we had a training and test dataset to gauge the correctness of our A.I. models. In unsupervised learning, we only have one dataset that we try to uncover insights and patterns from. These insights and patterns may not even be visible to the human eye, which makes these types of learning even more exciting.

If in supervised learning we were focused with approximation, here in unsupervised learning we are more focused with description. Our A.I. will learn to find conclusions by way of clustering, figuring out a distribution for the dataset, or even reducing dimensions to see the dataset just plotted in a 2D graph to see if there is structure. Given the scope of unsupervised learning, there are not a lot of models or tests that we can do. However, this does not necessarily make it useless, as entering something without assumptions and letting the facts speak for themselves can oftentimes lead us to better conclusions. Unsupervised learning is helpful since it creates outcomes for us regardless of our preconceived notions.

Reinforcement Learning

Right now, you are probably thinking to yourself, "that is not what I expected A.I. to be." Like what we said earlier, oftentimes when we think of A.I. we think of *Terminator*, *Ultron*, *the Matrix*, or any of those fancy Hollywood movies. To date, reinforcement learning is probably the closest thing we have to that vision of what A.I. looks like.

When we learn in real life, oftentimes we use a combination of both supervised and unsupervised learning. We have labeled datasets that we learn from, but at the same time, we have unlabeled datasets we work with to look for underlying structures or patterns that would help us better grasp the learning material at hand. However, the difference in both is the concept of time. Our time is a scarce resource, and we cannot keep learning forever. We have deadlines and other priorities that we must meet. As such, with each passing second, a penalty is imposed on us because that is a second that we could have used for a different task.

The thing that makes reinforcement learning (RL) powerful is this idea of incentive. Every move it makes has a corresponding incentive, think of it like points that you receive with every score. At the same time, penalties also exist in every move for the RL agent to be incentivized to move faster. It tries to maximize its expected future rewards by trying to look for an optimal way to perform a task at hand. A RL model gets thrown into an environment and is made to run multiple tests. It tries to answer questions like, "in state A, what action should I take? What does by total reward in the future look like? Is this really the right thing to do toward that goal?" In a way, you can say that it is like supervised learning since it the outcome is well defined. However, you can also say that it is unsupervised learning because it tries to look for patterns and structures within the environment without being fed the way to maximize future rewards beforehand. Somehow you can say it is the best of both worlds.

Which One to Use?

Each technique has its own unique way of characteristics that allow it to optimally solve a problem. However, let us dig a bit deeper and learn the different implementations from within those three. There are multitudes of supervised learning techniques, each with their own "fields of expertise." As such, for us to better solve problems right now, we need to first identify what type of problem is it and try to identify if it needs supervised, unsupervised, or reinforcement learning, then tap into the myriads of techniques within those three. Let us dive right in!

Supervised Learning

As we have discussed above, supervised learning is a "with help" type of learning. Our A.I. will learn a task at hand provided we give it the answers in the end. Again, this is like studying for a math test with practice tests and their corresponding answer keys. This is done to cross check how far or close our answers are from the solutions. When supervised learning A.I. model gets trained in real life, data usually needs to be cleaned and organized first.

PassengerId	Survived	Pclass	Name	Sex	Age	SibSp	Parch	Ticket	Fare	Cabin	Embarked
853 854	1	1	Lines, Miss. Mary Conover	female	16.0	0	1	PC 17592	39.4000	D28	S
232 233	0	2	Sjostedt, Mr. Ernst Adolf	male	59.0	0	0	237442	13.5000	NaN	S
409 410	0	3	Lefebre, Miss. Ida	female	NaN	3	1	4133	25.4667	NaN	S
693 694	0	3	Saad, Mr. Khalil	male	25.0	0	0	2672	7.2250	NaN	C

The above dataset is the infamous Titanic dataset. The dataset contains valuable information from the passengers of the Titanic like their name, age, sex, where their destination was, et al. But more importantly, the dataset also contains their survival status—0 if they died, while 1 if they survived.

This is what we call a *labeled* dataset. It is called labeled because it contains the column that is our objective. If our objective was to predict their survival status given all other information, and said information was available in the data, then we call it *labeled*. *Labeled* datasets are important because they contain information as to what our model is trying to predict.

The only difference between *labeled* and *unlabeled* data is the pre-defined target in mind—*labeled* datasets contain the information that we want our A.I. to predict. In *unlabeled* datasets, our targets are not decided yet, meaning we either do not know what we want our A.I. to predict or we just want to explore the contents and structure of the data at hand first.

The nature of the dataset is also reflective of how what learning method you will be using—*labeled* for supervised and *unlabeled* for unsupervised. More on this later.

If we were to predict if a person survived the titanic or not, then that would be considered as a classification problem. We are telling the A.I. to use all other features to figure out what type of passenger qualifies as a survivor or not. Since we are only concerned with either a dead or alive passenger, then the A.I. will try to figure out a *decision boundary* that defines what a survivor or a non-survivor looks like.

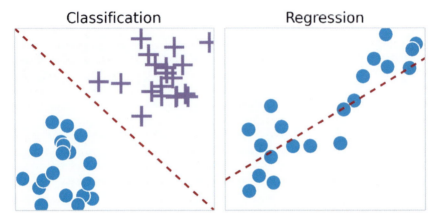

Source 1: http://ipython-books.github.io/images/ml.png

In the dataset, there are missing ages. Around 20% of them are missing. A technique called imputation could be used to fill in these missing values. A common method is to fill in the missing values with either the mean of the median. Some decide to use other factors such as first grouping them to where they embarked and then using either the mean or median of said groups to fill in the missing values. If a person embarked from Queenstown and the average or median age is X, then all persons with missing age values who embarked from Queenstown will now have age X.

However, another technique that can be utilized is regression. Assuming all other variables have non-empty values, then what a data scientist can do is to program an A.I. that first imputes missing age values given the other variables. This A.I. will predict what age group a person belongs to given trends present from other variables. This way, unlike the imputation method presented above, you take into consideration all other variables as well in determining the age of the person.

Regression can also be used for other things such as predicting market trends, likelihood of having a bad movie review, and all sorts of other applications. The same goes with classification. It is up to the imagination to figure out how creative an application can be.

Throughout your adventure in learning A.I., there will always be three supervised learning models that repeatedly show themselves: multilayer perceptrons, convolutional neural networks, and recurrent neural networks. Let us jump right in!

Multilayer Perceptron

Imagine the structure of your brain. You have millions, if not, billions of neurons firing every second as you obtain information in real time. Reading the newspaper? Neurons fire to bring back relevant information like similar occurrences or on-the-spot reactions and analyses. Practicing how to play the piano? Neurons fire relevant spots and strengthen their connections with practice over time. This is the inspiration that brought to life multilayer perceptrons (MLPs), neurons and strong connections with more practice.

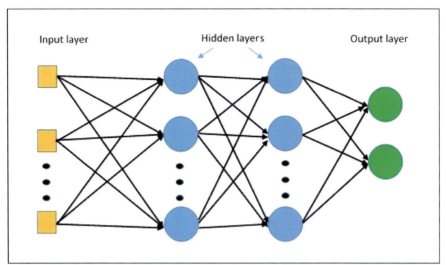

MLPs have three structures in them, namely the input layer, the hidden layer, and the output layer. The input layer contains all the relevant "features" that you need, the output layer is your goal, and the hidden layers are your nonlinear combinations of your hidden layers that handle deeper representation and abstraction. Each line was a certain weight that correspond to it. This weight determines how much one node influences another node. Much like in our own brains, if one node's functions does not directly relate to another node's function, then there is no need to strengthen their bond that pertains to playing the piano.

These weights are important because as the A.I. learns, it tweaks the values of these weights to create the proper neural pathways that define whatever it is the user wants to define. In our Titanic example, more refined paths will clearly define what it is that makes a Titanic survivor. This weight update is done through backpropagation, which is just a fancy way of saying chain rule. The simple idea behind backpropagation is that it spots the errors, and sends back those errors back to the network for it to make the necessary weight adjustments. With more training and more iterations of forward propagating the information and then backpropagating the error, the more the A.I. becomes better.

In the Titanic dataset, the input layer are the features you set that you think define a survivor and the output layer is the survived column. The hidden layer becomes the many different pool of ideas and combinations that will build up to the idea of what a Titanic survivor looks like. The beauty of the MLP is that its decision boundary becomes much complex compared to others. In the image earlier, we saw that the decision boundary was just a line. In the real world, data can become more complicated than that. A simple line will not suffice in those scenarios. Just look at the image below.

Neural Network Decision Boundary

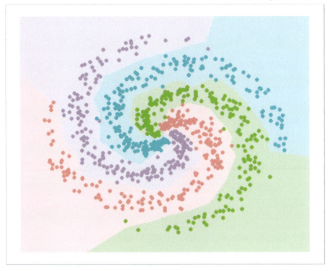

Source 3:
http://junma5.weebly.com/uploads/4/6/5/1/46519751/1241933_orig.png

Spiral decision boundaries are being made in response to the spiral nature of the dataset. A linear decision boundary cannot hope to accomplish the same level of elegance and complexity that an MLP can. These make MLPs versatile and powerful. Furthermore, this makes MLPs the building block of other A.I. models to come.

Convolutional Neural Network

Image classification has been around for a long time. Programming computers to recognize A from B has always been an interesting problem to solve. In the first iteration, lots of programmers would probably classify A from B based on their physical features. For example, in programming a "cats vs. dogs" classifier, there would be functions that would return whether or not the image has whiskers, paws, claws, a tail, and others. It would be tedious as there would be an endless stream of cat or dog features that you need to program. However, A.I. can just learn what it means to be a cat or a dog based on the data you feed it and make more accurate predictions from there.

The problem with just using MLPs is that they do not abstract deeper enough into what an image is. Furthermore, using MLPs is computationally explosive as the number of features explodes to whatever the dimension of the image is. If an image is 18x18 pixels, with 3 channels (red, blue and green), that would make 972 features in total. Furthermore, all nodes in one layer are connected to all the other nodes in the other layer. Imagine having 972 nodes in both the input and hidden layers. That means that nodes 1 to 972 in the input layer connects to all the other 972 nodes in the hidden layer. That is a lot. There should be a more efficient method.

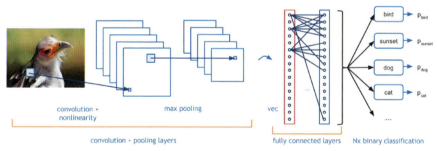

Source 4: https://adeshpande3.github.io/assets/Cover.png

CNNs, as they are otherwise called, reduces the dimensions while keeping the important features of an image intact. Imagine using a flashlight to illuminate a painting. You do not illuminate the entire thing, but just a small portion of the image from left to right—up to down. As you do this process of lighting up certain parts of the image, you are also only picking the most important features that you see, and transferring them over to somewhere else, creating a new image in the process. This is called max pooling.

12	20	30	0
8	12	2	0
34	70	37	4
112	100	25	12

2×2 Max-Pool →

20	30
112	37

Above we see an example of what max pooling does. The left square matrix is the numerical representation of our image while the size of the light of our flashlight is 2x2. As we move this 2x2 light across the image, we only get the most important feature, which in this case, corresponds to the biggest number. This spits out a new matrix from the right, which we either perform max pooling again or we now feed it into an MLP.

The MLP in this case gets the max pooling input that contains only the most relevant information. This is all the MLP needs, a dataset that contains the most important features, and then proceeds to create neural connections based off this. In a sense, it is like the Pareto principle of focusing on the 20% of inputs that produce 80% of the results. The convolution and max pooling parts figure out what that

20% of features is, while the MLP exploits that facts and learns from that as much as it can.

Recurrent Neural Network

Notice that since we started talking about supervised learning we have mostly been talking about sequence-independent examples. Image classification is not sequence-dependent. The same goes for either classifying surviving passengers or imputing missing age values with classification and regression respectively for MLPs. If we want to predict the movement of stock prices, or create a chat bot, then what should we use? RNNs, as they are often called, are our gems.

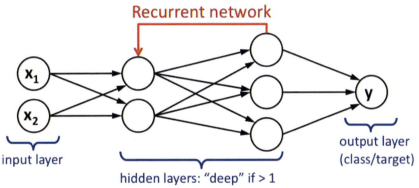

Source 6: https://leonardoaraujosantos.gitbooks.io/artificial-inteligence/content/image_folder_6/recurrent.jpg

Notice anything eerily familiar? Unlike the MLP, the hidden layer's last layer feeds its output back to the first layer of the hidden layer. This is the time component at work here. It does this based on the number of time steps defined in the dataset and then spits out a prediction in the output layer for your target time. Once you know how MLPs work, you pretty much know how RNNs work also. The one problem with RNNs is the vanishing/exploding gradient problem. The longer the time period, the more backpropagation has to reach back over time to make weight corrections. If the error values being sent back are too big, then the weight corrections explode. On the other hand, if the error values sent back are too small, then only the most recent ones benefit from the change, while the earlier ones get little to not benefit at all.

Another model called the long short-term memory (LSTM) network was created to address this problem. This model is another way of implementing an RNN that sidesteps the vanishing/exploding gradient altogether. All you need to know about this model is that, as the name implies, it far exceeds regular implementations of RNN because of not having to rely on gradients stacking up over time.

Possibilities

If you think about it, the possibilities with each of the discussed frameworks can be extended depending on how far you stretch them. MLPs, for example, are being used to classify and uncover what it means to get cancer or not. Meanwhile, CNNs are being used by Facebook for its facial recognition system. RNNs and LSTMs are being used for automated trading and generating text.

One smart example of using image recognition is MTailor, a Silicon Valley Startup who won a grant from Sam Altman's startup accelerator company called Y Combinator. You take a picture of yourself with the application and it determines the proper sizing of clothes for you just with that picture. This is an example of how to stretch the boundaries of imaginations that enables clever ways for A.I. to solve problems.

Another possibility for CNNs in the future may be house valuation. Just by taking key areas in the house, you can combine a CNN with an MLP to generate a price approximator. This way, when you are scouting for your new home, you can compare what the agent is offering and what the A.I. tells you is its approximate price. Extending the idea a bit further, let us a look at tis applications for car sales. An application that also approximates the price of a second-hand car might help people negotiate or even scout faster.

One last important application of RNNs and MLPs is fake news detection. By tweaking the necessary models under these two and combining natural language processing techniques, one could create a fake news detector. You would need a labeled dataset for this one, so creating the proper scale in which to rank the "realness" or "fakeness" of a news article will be a challenge.

Unsupervised Learning

Being able to tell A from B is one hallmark of intelligence. The hallmark present in supervised learning is the ability to improve one's understanding with repetition. Supervised learning can be boiled down to cost function minimization, since the minimum cost is most probably the optimum solution to our problem. For instance, we call people "gifted" or "genius level" since they are able to pick up things faster than usual. But the key idea there is that they are able to minimize future mistakes by spotting said mistakes earlier on. On the other hand, unsupervised learning highlights another hallmark of intelligence: the ability to tell apart things without prior context.

If in supervised learning we were concerning ourselves with approximations using regression and classification, we concern ourselves instead with descriptions in unsupervised learning using clustering and dimensionality reduction. As the name implies, unsupervised learning is "without help," utilizing unlabeled datasets, contrary to what supervised learning does.

Since there is no clear target in the dataset, unsupervised learning models are left to themselves to describe the natural structures that exist in data. Data scientists often create their own clusters beforehand based on their preconceptions and personal thoughts. However, there are times when there may exist a natural structure in the data that we may not have even been aware of. This structure is conceived upon about by our models' capabilities to comprehend endless amounts of dimensions and data, something that we humans are incapable of doing.

Clustering

As the name implies, clustering is all about lumping in together data based on similarities they share. Perhaps you lump student data based on their grades? Or maybe based on their extra-curricular activity?

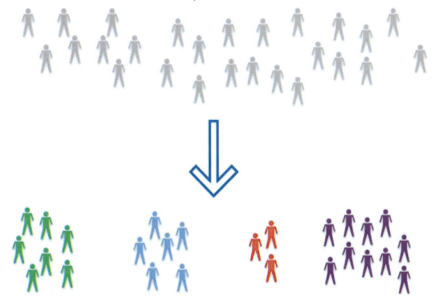

In the photo above we a clustering transformation from an unlabeled set of people to being clustered to four different groups. This is the power of unsupervised learning. It enables us to see which belongs which.

Imagine being a store owner and you wanted to utilize data science in order to better serve your customers. Since you know your business so well, you are well-equipped to make types of customers on the top of your head. Some might be students, some might be evening goers, Monday goers, et al. However, perhaps you notice that you are still not optimizing the amount of sales that you can make? That there are customers still that are left untapped that you cannot get your hands on? With enough customer data to use with unsupervised learning, you may be able to study who those customers are.

Two popular types of clustering methods are: 1) k-means clustering; and 2) Kohonen self-organizing maps (SOMs). Both do the same objective of clustering, but are different by nature.

The k in k-means is the number of clusters you want to partition the data into. For example, if you chose four clusters, then the final output will be four clusters. The problem with this is that you should know beforehand how many clusters you think exist. Perhaps you are thinking that defeats the purpose of clustering but it is not entirely the case. Assigning five clusters instead of four might lead to a different organization entirely. It is up to your creativity and inquisitiveness. However, different ks
may yield wishful thinking upon the data scientist. Proceed with caution. There are methods for finding out what the optimum number of clusters there are, but that is outside the scope of our discussion.

On the other hand, SOMs do not require assigning cluster numbers beforehand. It is less flexible than k-means in the sense that it will figure out the clusters on its own. What makes SOMs superior, in a sense, is its ability to maintain the structure of the data unlike k-means. What this means is that while SOMs traverse multidimensional space, their method of clustering data does not in any way change how close one data point is to another when moving translating it from one dimension to another. This preservation of structure is important since the natural structure of data is preserved in the clustering process, making your final clusters as natural as they can be.

Dimensionality Reduction

Clustering is fine and all but at the end of the day, we humans are visual creatures. It would be great if we could visually see what the clusters looked like.   Recall that the amount of dimensions that something has depends on the amount of features that you give it. For instance, using two features means being in two dimensions. But how do we visualize four, five, or even one hundred or more dimensions? As the name implies, dimensionality reduction involves reducing those dimensions to our desired number. Dimensionality reduction methods transform multidimensional data from one coordinate system to another.

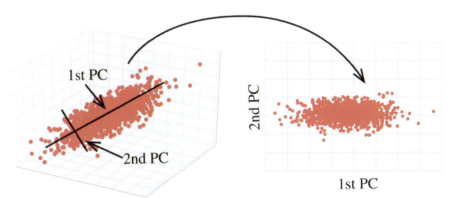

The importance of dimensionality reduction cannot be stressed enough. Sometimes it is best to see with our own eyes what the clusters look like. By visually inspecting, we can spend more time getting our own hands dirty with possible clusters or combinations of clusters.

Like clustering, there are two main methods used in dimensionality reduction, namely principal component analysis (PCA) and t-distributed stochastic neighbor embedding (t-SNE). Both are useful as they enable us to visualize N-dimensional data into to two- or three-dimensional space.

However, the devil is in the details, as they say. PCA mainly captures the linear structures between the features (columns in our spreadsheet) present in our data. This drawback causes the inaccurate transfer from higher to lower dimensional spaces. We say inaccurate because the structure from higher dimensions is not preserved in the dimensional reduction. This gets fixed when using t-SNE since, in this method, local distances are preserved within the higher to lower dimension mapping.

Possibilities

As long as we need to find clusters or understand the structure of data, unsupervised learning will get the job done. A practical application of this in the business world is customer profiling. Because of clustering, businesses are able to optimize their services based on which customer is which. For example, instead of blasting the same advertisements and promotions to every customer, a business would save much more money if they sent those to customers who fit the bill instead. If one cluster enjoys more of product or service A than B, then perhaps sending them discount codes or promotions on product or service A would be good for business and customer retention. This also means a lesser budget for the promotional bast, since the company will not be sending the discount to everyone.

Particle, star, or galaxy detection in physics requires an incredible amount of data. A faster way of looking for new types of particles, stars, or galaxies is by using unsupervised learning. The A.I. will tell you if a new cluster is forming and you can visualize it right away. You can spend less time this way investigating too much time on each new entry since you are only interested in new discoveries.

Reinforcement Learning

So far we have discussed ways an A.I. can learn either with or without help. Is there a way to combine the two? We humans use both all the time, so why do we have to use them separately for our A.I.? In reinforcement learning (RL), we use insights and techniques from both to model decision making processes.

The key to RL models is the concept of trial and error and their corresponding incentives. In the real world, we often repeat doing things that give us satisfaction, while we avoid things that give us pain or suffering. This explanation is vague for a reason. For example, grueling exercise to better your strength and speed is difficult and may even bring you to the brink of utter exhaustion. However, it may be that the reason people keep on doing it is the satisfaction that it brings them for the future, since with every repeat, they bring themselves closer to their fitness goals.

In real life, "satisfaction" is subjective as it depends from person to person. In RL however, we get to define what constitutes "satisfaction" and what does not. In a first-person shooter game, a game bot programmed with RL may define satisfaction as the amount of kills made from the opposing team, while its number of deaths are defined as not being satisfactory. The main insight is that actions that give us satisfying results are more likely to be repeated than those that offer no satisfaction whatsoever.

If you have not noticed by now, most of the insights we get from our understanding of how we learn gets transformed into math, including decision making. However, our mathematical interpretations are never completely accurate, which is why an iterative process of trial and error is done in order to check what we are lacking and figure out a way to fix that.

Markov Decision Process

Decision making can be said as a generalization of both supervised and unsupervised learning. Informed decisions are those that are learned through multiple iterations of supervised learning. More examples mean greater opportunities to learn from past mistakes to improve upon in the future. When left to one's own devices, making decisions based on "hunches" or "gut feeling" can be said to mirror unsupervised learning. Deciding on something by being able to see patterns or structures is something we do when thrown into a new situation. RL is as close as we can get right now to actual AGI.

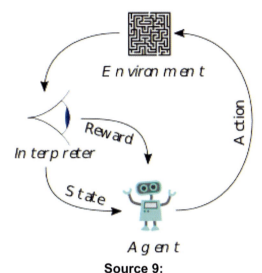

Source 9:
https://upload.wikimedia.org/wikipedia/commons/thumb/1/1b/Reinfor cement_learning_diagram.svg/250px-Reinforcement_learning_diagram.svg.png

The markov decision process (MDP) is at the centerpiece of most RL models. MDP is a mathematical framework used for decision making where said decisions are part-random and part-under control by the agent. MDPs are defined by a set of states, actions, rewards, and transitions. For example, playing tic-tac-toe can be modeled using MDP. For each state, you have certain actions that you can take. Each action that you take grants you an award of some sort, whether it is gaining an edge on your opponents or winning the game itself.

The goal of the game agent is to find a policy that results in the greatest future rewards. This policy is something that you learn through experience. Given a scenario, because of past experiences, you would know what to do. For example, when you are in city X past midnight, do you take route A or B? Experience helps in your decision making process because you would know by then what the proper course of action should be.

The beauty about the MDP is that it also works for non-deterministic situations. These are situations in which "going up" or "pressing the button" do not necessarily result in the desired outcome. For example, maybe "going up" is only 80% probable, while "going down" is 10% probable, and "going left" and "going right" are each 5% probable.

4x3 Grid World

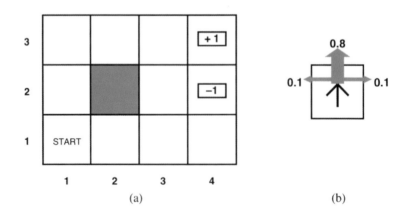

(a)　　　　　　　　　　(b)

The image above is an environment that has a total of 12 states in the 4x3 grid. An agent also has four moves, namely up, down, left, and right. But because of stochasticity, which is a fancy way of saying being probabilistic, the supposed consequence of certain actions are never certain. This is also the case in real life. For example, when we are playing basketball, shooting from the three-point line may not always result in a field goal. Or to be more specific, shooting under your most favorable conditions—however they may be defined—do not always yield the result you want. You may be wide open for a three-point shot while being "on fire" the entire game, but that does not mean that the shot is assured to go in. There is always a chance it might not, and we do not have control over that chance.

(Deep) Q-Learning

When creating RL agents, we want them to be as independent as to a game as possible. We call Q-learning as a "model-free" RL technique. These techniques that we subject our RL agents to use as their medium for training must be generalizable. Recall that earlier, intelligence is not only defined as the ability to recall past knowledge, but also the ability to apply the same methods to other subject matters as well. This is where Q-learning steps into play.

Convolutional Agent

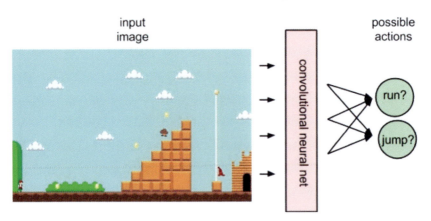

Source 11: https://leonardoaraujosantos.gitbooks.io/artificial-inteligence/content/deep_reinforcement_learning.html

The "Q" in Q-learning can be thought of as "quality." Certain combinations of state and action yield a "quality" to them—often denoted by a number with the highest one having the highest quality. For example, in basketball, it may make more sense to shoot the ball when you are wide open and in your "sweet spot." Which action to take is dictated by whatever our policy is for a given state. The beauty about Q-learning is that it handles stochastic situations pretty well without need for model-specific adjustments. Q-learning also converges to an optimal solution, meaning training does not get stuck in a loop.

However, to improve Q-learning, we have to make it deep. Much like in DNNs where hidden layers represent deeper abstraction of ideas, making our Q-learning deeper will allow for better learning, and more often than not, be more creative in making moves. This is where we finally introduce the deep Q-network (DQN)

Let us use game bots for our example. RL is widely used for creating game bots because they are the closest to mimicking real world scenarios. As inputs, we can take in pixel values. A familiar model we have already discussed is the CNN. However, unlike earlier, we do not use max pooling since adding it makes our CNN spatially invariant. Max pooling is fine if you are doing classification, but for our purposes, we need our RL agent to be sensitive to the location in each given pixel values. The only difference between Q-learning and DQNs is that the latter utilizes more layers of CNNs and DNNs as can be seen in the picture below.

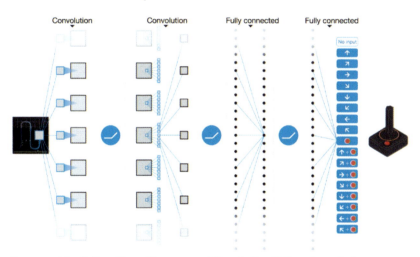

Source 12: https://medium.com/@awjuliani/simple-reinforcement-learning-with-tensorflow-part-4-deep-q-networks-and-beyond-8438a3e2b8df

Current State of RL

Right now RL research is hot between Google's DeepMind and Sam Altman and Elon Musk's OpenAI. Both are world renowned research organizations that focus all their energy on A.I. research. Both organizations seek to advanced A.I. research by creating machines that can learn without the need to be taught. The beauty of RL is that it can be completely bad at what it does in the beginning, while a week later, become a complete expert on what it is you programmed it to do. This is a powerful approach compared to supervised learning, where you have to spoon-feed your models the answers in order for it to minimize future errors.

Google DeepMind's most famous success is having their program called AlphaGo defeat world-renowned Go player Lee Sedol from South Korea four times in a five-game series. This is the first time a program was able to beat a high-ranking Go player without any handicaps. This marked a foundation to which we can apply our current RL implementations when stretched far enough.

Sam Altman and Elon Musk's OpenAI also had its recent fair share of the spotlight when their DotA game bot beat world class player Dendi in a 1v1 battle during the international DotA 2 tournament. Chief Technical Officer Greg Brockman explained that their game bot was trained to play against itself for two weeks. It is amazing how their game bot only took weeks to become world class in playing DotA when these other world class players took years of hard work.

OpenAI has since released an open-source library called Gym, which is a collection of different games that a developer can play around with. By democratizing access to this library,

OpenAI has made RL development a competition by seeing which machines score better. This will rapidly increase RL development as more unique solutions are generated every day.

Possibilities

Game bots are only the beginning. They serve as a foundation with what RL can do as they mimic what can happen in real life. An immediate practical use for RL is in self-driving cars. Tesla is currently using RL and other neural network-based algorithms to better their self-driving cars. By making RL agents train on simulations first, or from having them observe actual drivers, their learning can accelerate.

The benefit of having an RL-based driver is hivemind communication. Human drivers communicate poorly with other drivers on the road for obvious reasons. By nature, we tend to be easily distracted in most scenarios. One moment we may be dozing off into the sunset when we are driving back home, and the other moment we are so laser-focused on our driving so as to avoid being tangled in an accident. As for RL-based drivers? No such variability occurs. A network of communicating A.I. is much faster and less prone to miscommunication than one driver trying to tell the driver two cars away to move it. One can imagine the traffic inefficiencies will eventually be smoothed out as machines are the ones communicating in this hivemind.

Apart from self-driving cars, there is also surgery. It sounds far-fetched now because we would need to run more tests over time, but we are marginally getting close. Imagine a robot performing surgery with absolute precision with its scalpel. It does not shake, get nervous, or suffer from fatigue. If a DotA game bot can become world-class in two weeks time, imagine what surgery-related RL research can do if they train it for a year.

Another exciting application for RL is in customer service. Chat bots also count in RL research if we include natural language processing into the mix. A company can cut its expenditures by instead hiring bots to chat with customers on social media or talk to customers calling in via phone. These bots will be able to give answers quickly and will not be worried with an influx of customers trying to get a response all at the same time. Much like self-driving cars and surgery, these bots also do not suffer from fatigue, meaning they can work 24/7.

RL-based agents can help automating a lot of jobs that: 1) requires less than a few seconds to think or do; or 2) ones where fatigue becomes a factor over time. The possibilities are endless so as long as the imagination and creativity are boundless.

Moving Forward

Congratulations! You now have a high-level understanding of how most modern A.I. implementations work. This is great because this means that there is no need to fear A.I. as much anymore. The more we understand how a piece of technology works, the less of the unknown exists. It is this unknown that causes fear—we fear things we do not understand. When before, humans feared photographs because of the belief that cameras captured the soul, now we have social media websites that thrive on sharing photos and experiences to a vast majority of people.

As with any piece of technology, it is the users and developers that ultimately determine if they are going to be used for good or bad. A knife can only be as good as the person who wields it. Most people use knives to aid in cooking, but others use it to commit acts of horror. The same goes for A.I. and other computer programs.

To illustrate the point further, a hacker is not necessarily bad. Some hackers work for companies to find holes in securities. These hackers get paid to fix these holes so that both company and customer privacy is better secured. On the other hand, there are also hackers out there who use their skills to steal information and wealth. Does this make hacking a bad thing? It does not. It is the people who use such skills that make it bad, not the skill in of itself.

A.I. can be framed in a similar fashion. RL-based machines that will kill in a warzone without hesitation, CNNs that are used for criminal profiling, clustering methods that weed out one group from another, any many others. As has been said many times, the possibilities are endless so as long as imagination and creativity are boundless, but that does not mean that they lead to good outcomes.

Another possible concern is the "runaway A.I." like *Terminator* or *Ultron*. But here is the thing, we are still far away from that. As we have seen time and time again, our current A.I. implementations are only able to generalize within the domain it was trained to learn on. Having an A.I. that will take over the world like how they depict it in Hollywood is still a far-away idea.

However, there are close scenarios concerning "runaway A.I." that may mimic end-of-the-world scenarios. For example, if we have our A.I. run a country's weapons systems, and we optimize that A.I. to only launch those weapons to the "biggest threats" to that country's freedom, then there might be a chance it will go for a suicide instead. Or worse, if not trained properly, it might launch those weapons to allies or other innocent countries. Since we cannot intuitively interpret hidden layers or deep abstractions that our A.I. undergoes, this will be harder to solve than it seems. One solution might be to "plug it off" the system. However, what if it learns to leave traces of itself into the system like a virus? It gets tricky dealing with these kinds of things.

One real life example of a "runaway A.I." is Facebook's news feed. The news feed was set to optimize for attention so that users spend time surfing through it. However, problems like political division widen because of this. Since it wants to optimize the user's attention, then it will only show material that pertain to reinforcing the user's political leanings. It does not make sense to show material that counteract that. This is an unintended consequence that resulted from the A.I.'s intrinsic values not aligning with its creators.

Are we doomed? Not necessarily. The solution lies in laying out a set of practices for creating A.I. that align their intrinsic values with ours. OpenAI is leading the charge toward outlining these practices. But it should not be just them. Anyone with an interest in A.I. can join in on the discussion and pitch in ideas. Having a free market of ideas where one idea clashes with another is a good way of finding out which ideas work best. As we have read earlier, a lot of the breakthroughs in A.I. came from intuitions found outside of it. You do not need to be a math genius.

Another thing we can do is to further educate the public on A.I. and how it works. The more people understand how these things work, the more they become aware of how they can be used for nefarious purposes, and direct things like advocacy and policy in the right direction. We all have a stake in this. If A.I. is not used properly, then we are all going to get inevitably affected by it. However, if A.I. is used properly, then that can only lead to more prosperity and problems solved.

31013764R00028

Printed in Poland
by Amazon Fulfillment
Poland Sp. z o.o., Wrocław